A Home by the Sea

W9-CNA-248

A Home by the Sea

PROTECTING COASTAL WILDLIFE

Kenneth Mallory

A New England Aquarium Book

A Gulliver Green Book

Harcourt Brace & Company

San Diego   New York   London

Library of Congress Cataloging-in-Publication Data
Mallory, Kenneth.
A home by the sea: protecting coastal wildlife/Kenneth Mallory.
p.   cm.
"A New England Aquarium Book."
"A Gulliver Green Book."
Summary: Describes programs being carried out in New Zealand to protect coastal animals such as dolphins and penguins which are being threatened by development.
ISBN 0-15-200043-7   ISBN 0-15-201802-6 pb
ISBN 0-8172-5766-7 (Library binding)
1. Wildlife conservation—New Zealand—Juvenile literature.
2. Coastal animals—New Zealand—Juvenile literature.
[1. Wildlife conservation.   2. Marine animals.
3. New Zealand.]   I. Title.
QL84.7.N45M35. 1998
333.95'416'0993—dc21 97-38020

First edition
F E D C B A
F E D C B A (pb)

Printed in Singapore

The author would like to acknowledge the following people for their help in creating this book: Robin Burliegh, Viv Hextall, Alistair (the-gloves-are-off) Hutt, Ellie Linen, Stephanie Martin, Hiltrun Ratz, Steve Robb, Greg Stone, and Austen Yoshinaga. And finally, I would like to thank Jerry R. Schubel, president of the New England Aquarium, who inspired in me and countless others an appreciation for the rhythms of the coast.

Photo Credits
All photographs are by Kenneth Mallory except as follows. Greg Stone: p. 2, p. 6 (upper left inset), pp. 7–10, pp. 15–16, p. 17 (top and right), pp. 18–19, p. 20 (left), p. 21, p. 24 (right), p. 25, p. 26 (top), pp. 32–34, p. 62. Scott Kraus: p. 12 (top and left). Paul Erickson: p. 13. Satellite image of Banks Peninsula on p. 14 courtesy NASA.

Map on p. 18 by Patti Isaacs, Parrot Graphics

Gulliver Green® books focus on various aspects of ecology and the environment, and a portion of the proceeds from the sale of these books is donated to protect, preserve, and restore native forests.

Designed by Ivan Holmes

This book is dedicated to the diversity of life on our planet, and to the people who care enough to preserve it.

Introduction

"In the end we will conserve only what we love, we will love only what we understand, and we will understand only what we are taught."

—Baba Dioum, a Senegalese philosopher

Above: *Little blue penguins in their shore-line habitat at Banks Peninsula, South Island, New Zealand*

Left: *A view of Boston Harbor showing congested shoreline development*

Insets: *A pair of Hector's dolphins at play, and an adult yellow-eyed penguin*

A little blue penguin, caught in an oil slick, flounders to shore and a likely death; a dolphin the length of a bicycle gets trapped in a fishing net intended to catch cod and butterfish and nearly drowns; a yellow-eyed penguin wanders in confusion, searching in vain for a safe nesting site in a tract of newly constructed seaside homes. The dangers these animals face are as different as the animals themselves, but the reason for the danger is always the same: There are too many people competing with the animals for a place to call home.

These animals and others are finding their living spaces invaded and shrinking at an alarming rate. If human population growth continues at its present pace—ten thousand people every hour of every day—within thirty years more than 7 billion people will live within 50 miles of a coast. Coastal-dwelling animals are on a collision course with the 5- to 6-foot-tall mammals we call humans.

We are all looking for a place to live.

A thousand miles from its nearest neighbor, Australia, New Zealand stands as a shining example of what can be done to protect our endangered coastal animals and their habitats. At all levels in New Zealand, people are working to preserve its wide variety of native wildlife—what is called its *biodiversity.* Scientists are working with local interests to ensure species survival, conservationists are creating habitat sanctuaries, and grass-roots groups are turning homes into halfway stations for emergency animal care. Together, these programs form a package that protects endangered wildlife. The success New Zealand has had in preserving its biodiversity shows us the kind of effort we all must make so that animals *and* people can live peacefully side by side on Earth far into the future.

Left: *Marine mammal curator Kathy Krieger Streeter takes her first look at Hector's dolphins swimming alongside her research boat.*

Opposite: *Underwater view of a Hector's dolphin*

How Science Is Helping the Hector's Dolphin

New England Aquarium biologist Greg Stone has always been fascinated by whales.

His curiosity about them has taken him all over the world, from the frigid polar waters of the Antarctic to the crystal clear depths of the Sargasso Sea near Bermuda to the mist-shrouded currents off New Zealand's South Island coast. He has followed the migration of 50-foot-long humpback mothers and their 15-foot-long calves from the Antarctic to the coast of Ecuador and Peru, and has swum with playful dolphins off the coast of Japan. But when the New Zealand Department of Conservation requested his help, he had a once-in-a-lifetime opportunity: He was asked to study a whale even smaller than he is, the Hector's dolphin.

Hector's dolphins grow to an average of just over 4 feet long, a third the length of the more familiar bottlenose dolphin. Size, color patterns, and the shape of its fins distinguish a Hector's dolphin from its other dolphin and porpoise cousins. Overall, its body is gray and white except for a wash of black pigment that sweeps from the tip of one pectoral fin, across its eyes, and to the pectoral fin on the other side, making it look as though the Hector's dolphin is wearing a faded black mask. But what helps researchers most in recognizing a Hector's dolphin is the dorsal fin on the top of its back: On most other dolphins this fin is sharply crescent-shaped, but on the Hector it is gently rounded.

Above: *A solitary Hector's dolphin shows the characteristic rounded dorsal fin on its back. The shape of this fin helps distinguish the Hector's from other dolphin species.*

Opposite: *This leaping or breaching Hector's dolphin reveals the black mask and other color patterns of a typical Hector's.*

A Dolphin Is a Whale with Porpoise

We often think of science as "exact" and "factual," as a source of knowledge that delivers the "truth" and gives final answers with precise language. But science is much messier than that. Science is a process, a way of trying to make sense of nature even as new facts emerge and a different interpretation of the facts is applied. The confusion about whether a marine mammal is a whale, a dolphin, or a porpoise is a good example. Even as this is written, there is discussion among whale biologists whether the terms *dolphin* and *porpoise* should be used at all. Until recently, it has made sense to distinguish these two kinds of toothed whales by their teeth (porpoise teeth are spade-shaped; dolphin teeth are cone-shaped) and their beaks (porpoises do not have beaks; dolphins do). But Hector's "dolphins" are one of a number of examples that contradict this model, since they are a dolphin in all respects except they don't have a beak.

And it gets even more confusing. Most dolphins are mammals, but there is a large

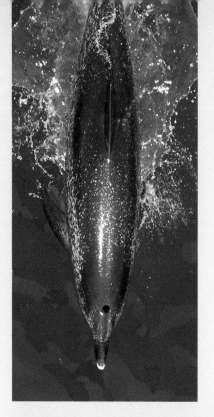

dolphin of tropical waters that is a fish: It's called the dolphin fish or dorado, grows 5 feet long, and in Hawaii is a premium eating fish called mahimahi. How do we avoid confusion between the mammal and the fish?

And what about whales? Does the term *whale* only refer to the large, primarily baleen whales of the ocean, or does it also include dolphins and porpoises? On this issue, however, there is agreement: About the only definition almost everyone agrees on is that dolphins and porpoises are whales, and that they belong to a marine mammal order called Cetacea.

Left: *The pronounced beak and conical teeth of a typical dolphin*

Above: *The beak that usually distinguishes dolphins from porpoises is clearly visible in this view of a dolphin just after it has surfaced.*

Right: *The beak of this harbor porpoise is typically more blunt than its dolphin cousins.*

Above: *Two white-sided dolphins rehabilitated in a special tank at the New England Aquarium show the typical crescent-shaped fins and characteristic dolphin beak.*

Understanding and preserving wild animal populations is complicated. Conservation biologists like Greg Stone have to see every side of an issue and must be part diplomat, part biologist, part politician, part native and commercial fisherman, part world citizen—even part dolphin. Greg was an independent voice, and he knew a tremendous amount about dolphins: just what the New Zealand Department of Conservation needed to fairly sort out the many claims and interests in the future of the Banks Peninsula sanctuary.

In 1989, when Greg first arrived at Banks Peninsula with his wife and co-researcher Austen Yoshinaga, he already knew Hector's dolphins were in trouble. The results of a four-year survey by New Zealand scientists Stephen Dawson and Elisabeth Slooten showed that Hector's dolphins lived in population clumps, often separated by great distances. If some disaster struck one of these small population centers, it might not have enough animals to recover, and that population of dolphins might slowly dwindle and die out.

Through hillside observations and a series of census-taking boat excursions along the coast, Slooten and Dawson were able to map out how the dolphin population was distributed around the islands. One population cluster was a relatively small group off New Zealand's North Island, the second a much larger group on the west coast of South Island, and yet a third cluster of animals was off Banks Peninsula on the east coast of South Island.

Left: *A satellite photo of Banks Peninsula showing the inlet leading to Akaroa Harbor*

Opposite: *The view near Akaroa Harbor on Banks Peninsula*

14

Although the overall Hector's dolphin population was estimated to be three to four thousand, the number around the peninsula was only 740 individuals. Of this number, an alarming 230 appeared to have been killed in fishermen's nets between 1984 and 1988. By the time Greg arrived in 1989 the cluster's population was thought to have dwindled to 510, a dangerously small number for maintaining a healthy breeding stock.

The numbers were discouraging. Hector's dolphin females don't give birth to their first calf until they are seven to nine years old. They can produce a calf every two to three years, and they might be expected to live to a maximum of twenty years. When survival rates were figured into the equation, Dawson and Slooten estimated the best yearly increase in dolphins would be 2 percent of the overall population. In other words, the Banks Peninsula group might increase by fifteen animals each year. But the group

Above: *Hector's dolphins give birth every two to three years. The young calf here has what are called fetal folds, vertical stripes that are reminders of the folded fetal position it was in before birth.*

Top: A *fishing boat is docked at Akaroa Harbor, Banks Peninsula.*

Above: *This type of fishing net, along with gill nets, is sometimes responsible for accidental deaths of Hector's dolphins.*

Top right: *The body of a Hector's dolphin has washed up on a beach in Akaroa Harbor, New Zealand.*

was losing nearly fifty-eight per year from fishing nets. At this rate Hector's dolphins would vanish from the Banks Peninsula area in as few as fifteen years.

The cause of the dolphin deaths was the practice of suspending nets—called gill nets or set nets—like a curtain or wall sometimes a hundred feet long floating just above the bottom of the ocean. Though fishermen intended the nets only to catch fish inside the bays and inlets around Banks Peninsula, set nets sometimes also caught and drowned dolphins by accident.

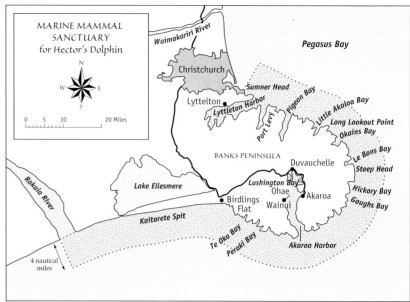

Because of the Hector's dolphin deaths, in 1988 the New Zealand government had declared the area around Banks Peninsula extending 2.4 miles out into the ocean to be a marine mammal sanctuary. The sanctuary was formed to keep commercial fishermen away from important Hector's dolphin breeding grounds. It was also designed to limit recreational fishermen from setting nets during heavy dolphin traffic season from November through February. The designation of the sanctuary pleased environmentalists but met fierce resistance from the fishing and tourist community.

Commercial and recreational fishermen questioned the accuracy of the Hector's dolphin death toll. They also questioned whether the deaths were really caused by the fishing nets. And local businesses worried about a downturn in tourism because recreational fishermen bought homes, used local campgrounds, and spent their money in local restaurants and gas stations while vacationing in the area. Finding a solution that satisfied everyone was an important reason the New Zealand Department of

Left: A story in the local New Zealand newspaper documents the death of Hector's dolphins in and around Banks Peninsula.

Above: A map shows the location and boundary of the Marine Mammal Sanctuary for Hector's dolphins near Banks Peninsula.

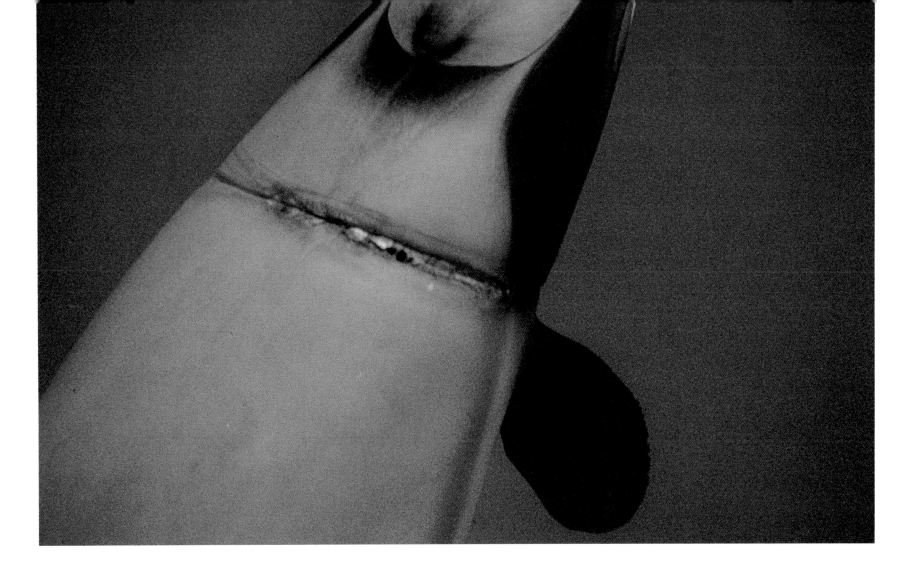

Conservation needed Greg's independent evaluation. His was an outside voice that could tell them how effectively the sanctuary was working and whether a complete ban on fishing was necessary.

If researchers could better understand the dolphins' movement patterns, the government might be able to better manage fishing in the future so both fishermen and dolphins could share the resources of the harbors without endangering the dolphins.

Above: The circle around this Hector's dolphin's head is a wound made by a fishing line. Accidental entrapment in fishing gear causes the deaths of thousands of whales worldwide and was the reason for the commercial fishing ban around Akaroa Harbor.

Greg knew it was important to understand how Hector's dolphins used the major inlets in Banks Peninsula and why they were caught in fishermen's nets as they were traveling back and forth. To get the kind of information he needed, Greg set up viewing stations on the high hills of Akaroa (ak-ah-ROW-ah) Harbor, the biggest inlet on the Banks Peninsula.

Cliff-top observers worked in teams of two researchers, one scanning the harbor for dolphins, the other taking notes. By watching from the cliffs, the scientists could observe the dolphins without the dolphins' knowledge and so would see natural, unaffected behaviors. Dolphins, like people, act differently when they know they are being watched.

From their three different vantage points over Akaroa Harbor, the scientists began to see a pattern. The dolphins moved inshore in the early morning and remained there until afternoon and evening, when they began moving out of the harbor. Where they went at night, however, was still a mystery, despite a short trial of observations using night-vision goggles.

Left: *Researcher Austen Yoshinaga observes movement of Hector's dolphins in and out of the inlet leading to Akaroa Harbor, Banks Peninsula.*

Above: *Greg Stone with the night-vision goggles he used to track nighttime migration of Hector's dolphins*

Opposite: *Two Hector's dolphins in the calm waters around Akaroa Harbor. Much of Greg Stone's research focused on the movement of Hector's dolphins in and out of Akaroa Harbor.*

In the process of scientific problem solving, when one approach to getting information doesn't answer the questions researchers pose, they design a better approach. Since he couldn't see the dolphins at night, Greg came up with a different way to follow them.

Whale scientists use a "tag" to track the movement of animals in the wild. In one of its most successful forms, a radio transmitter, or tag, is attached to the dorsal fin of a whale. The tag emits radio signals whenever the animal comes to the surface to breathe. The signals tell onlookers where an animal surfaces and how long it stays underwater. With the Hector's dolphin, however, Greg had a problem: How could he place a tag on the animal without causing it harm?

Opposite: *A harbor porpoise is tagged before release in Boston Harbor after convalescence at the New England Aquarium.*

Right: *Radio and satellite tags attached to the dorsal fin of a pilot whale prior to release*

The New England Aquarium had successfully placed transmitters on large pilot whales and white-sided dolphins by bolting the radio tag in place and designing it to rust off naturally a few weeks later. The aquarium's veterinarian drilled small holes in the whales' dorsal fins in a process similar to piercing a human ear for earrings. But the Hector was much smaller than previously tagged whales and might be hurt by the drill. Greg decided to attach a tag by means of a 3-inch suction cup rather than drill a hole.

Greg had already tested the suction-cup tags on the back of one of the other researchers—and his test subject still came to work the next day—so Greg knew the tag wouldn't harm the dolphins. Encouraged by this success, Greg set out. As his small research boat pulled alongside a group of dolphins playing in its wake, Alistair Hutt, a New Zealand conservation officer who was working with Greg, would poke a 5-foot-long pole, spring-loaded with the suction tag, onto the back of the nearest dolphin.

Left: A radio tag with the suction cup that holds it to the dolphin's back and the tiny device that emits radio signals

Above: Researchers use a pole to attach suction-cup radio tags to Hector's dolphins.

Above: *A leaping Hector's dolphin displays a radio suction tag successfully attached to its flank.*

The suction tags worked beautifully. The results confirmed a pattern of early morning visits to the harbor and late afternoon and early evening movement back out to sea. The dolphins were probably chasing schools of fish as they entered the harbor during the day.

25

Playing High-Tech Tag

For decades now, scientists who track animals that live on the land have been getting information about the daily lives of their study animals from radio and satellite "tags." Researchers place tags on endangered wood storks in the Everglades that beep coded information up to satellites, which in turn relay the details to computers sitting in research laboratories. A radio tag attached to a collar on a Siberian tiger tells scientists which water hole their research animal visited late yesterday evening. Tagging is a commonplace and easy way to keep tabs on a species.

But putting tags on animals that live in the water has never been quite so easy.

The New England Aquarium in Boston, Massachusetts, has been one of a small number of aquariums that has made a commitment to rescuing and tagging marine mammals such as harbor seals, and then releasing the animals back to the wild. In the 1970s, the aquarium glued radio tags to the heads of harbor seals—tags that sent VHF (very high frequency) radio beeps to research vessels.

Radio tags give information about the location of an animal as it moves through water as much as 5 miles away (or about as far as the eye can see). Similar radio tag devices allowed aquarium staff to follow white-sided dolphins off the fishing area called Georges Bank and harbor porpoises as they explored a path around Boston Harbor.

Satellite tags—usually bigger and bulkier than their radio tag cousins—offer the next step in information gathering. A satellite tag on one of three pilot whales named Baby, Tag, and Notch, rescued from a mass stranding on a Cape Cod, Massachusetts, beach,

allowed aquarium researchers to track the animals for three months when they were released off the coast of Massachusetts. The tag showed where they went, the number of times they dived, and the depths they reached on their daily search for food.

Then, in 1996, a hooded seal strayed far from its usual haunts in the Arctic Circle and ended up on a small beach north of Boston. Stephanie, as she was called, was released with a satellite tag epoxied to her fur. Stephanie's release caused quite a stir—not because the satellite tag she carried was a giant step in the use of tagging technology, but

Above: *Greg Stone monitoring dolphins at a tracking station set high on the hills of Banks Peninsula to pick up VHF radio signals from tags placed on dolphins*

Left: *Tagging a right whale*

26

because she was followed daily by tens of thousands of schoolchildren and Internet-savvy adults through a site called WhaleNet (http://whale.wheelock.edu).

WhaleNet and its Satellite Tagging Observation Program is an innovative educational Web page that helps viewers construct mapping profiles of where Stephanie, a pair of blue whales, and a North Atlantic right whale named Metompkin have traveled.

What is the future of tagging animals in the ocean? We have already caught a glimpse. Small capsules placed in the stomach of a harbor seal detect temperature changes that indicate when and how often the animal feeds. The stomach tag communicates with a satellite tag glued to the fur on the harbor seal's back, and that tag in turn communicates with an orbiting satellite and ultimately to a scientist's computer. Archival

tags about 2 inches long and half an inch thick are now put into the skin of a large ocean-migrating bluefin tuna and, when the animal is caught on the other side of the ocean and the tag recovered, months of research data are recovered for data-hungry scientists and fishermen. And finally, for perhaps the ultimate thrill in seagoing

adventure, engineer Graham Hawkes has recently completed a prototype of Deep Rover, a submersible that can travel fast enough underwater to shadow the every movement of a humpback whale.

As tagging technology improves, endangered animal species such as the yellow-eyed penguin

and the Hector's dolphin have a lot to gain. Information from the animals' daily travels can help scientists find ways to increase their chances for survival. And the better we understand how animals move through the oceans, the better we will be able to tailor our uses of the oceans so that we don't interfere with the wildlife there.

Right: A harbor porpoise is gently lifted from its temporary home at the New England Aquarium in preparation for tagging and release.

Greg knew information about dolphin swimming patterns would be a great help to the New Zealanders managing the sanctuary. Of even greater value, however, would be some way to scare dolphins away from fishing nets *before* they became entangled and drowned. The fishermen could then continue the business of fishing while the dolphins remained unharmed. Drawing on the success the New England Aquarium had scaring harbor porpoises away by attaching pingers—battery-powered devices that produce *beep-beep* sounds—to fishermen's nets in the North Atlantic Ocean, Greg began a summer of trial experiments in 1996 using pingers in Akaroa Harbor.

It might seem strange that an animal equipped with powerful sonar for locating underwater objects could ever get trapped in a net. But Greg suspected that Hector's dolphins don't keep their sonar running all the time. It is when they get careless and turn their sonar off that they get into trouble. A constantly operating pinger attached to fishing nets might force the dolphins to pay attention and stop them from blundering into the net.

Alistair Hutt took the inner tube from the tire of one of his trucks and filled it with air to make it into a floating platform. The platform would in turn serve as the base for a

Opposite: Research assistants Stephanie Martin and Ellie Linen prepare a pinger apparatus for deployment in the waters near Akaroa Harbor.

Right: A makeshift, battery-powered gearbox that lowers and raises beeping pingers into and out of the water

Far right: A rubber inner tube from a truck tire is the platform for an experiment using pingers to warn dolphins of the presence of fishing nets. The pinger hangs in the water dangling from the inner tube.

motorized pulley system to dangle the pinger into the water at the end of a fishing line. Greg made sure the observers on the hilltops never knew whether the pinger was active or not. This way, observations about whether the dolphins moved toward or away from the pinger wouldn't be influenced by knowing whether the pinger was on or off. Weeks and weeks of dolphin surveying was required to help Greg and the other scientists draw conclusions as to whether the "pinging" kept Hector's dolphins away or not.

By the end of March 1996, Greg had recorded enough observations of the pingers in action to conclude they were a resounding success. Although pingers didn't drive the dolphins out of the harbor, they did discourage their approach, and thus showed great promise for future use on commercial fishing nets. Only further tests on actual fishing vessels and their nets will tell whether pingers like these become a required feature of coastal fishing.

Of course, one of the biggest questions the New Zealand government wanted to answer was how effectively the sanctuary was doing what it was designed to do: save dolphins. Based on reports of fishermen who were required to report accidental take of dolphin in their nets, the sanctuary was working the way they hoped it would. In the first eight years of fishing controls, only a few dolphin deaths were reported. And the Hector's population appeared to be stable and maybe even increasing.

Opposite: *Research assistants deploy survey equipment to track and monitor movement of Hector's dolphins in and out of the inlet leading to Akaroa Harbor.*

Thanks to fishing restrictions and, in the future, devices like pingers, Hector's dolphins and humans can both use Akaroa Harbor. But perhaps the most important dilemma of all remains to be resolved.

If there are three to four thousand Hector's dolphins clumped in separate groups throughout New Zealand, are all of these groups still the same species? Or have they lived apart from one another for so long that evolution has made them different, unable to breed with one another?

If this is the true picture for these dolphins, and if a major disaster occurred to the group of dolphins in and around Akaroa Harbor, the number of dolphins of the same species would be even smaller than scientists had thought and dangerously close to extinction. Only careful work to identify the genetic material—the DNA—of each population cluster will determine just how different the geographically separated groups have become. Scientists have now turned their attention to understanding the true nature of the different Hector's population clusters and figuring out how best to protect them.

Left: *A fishing vessel near Banks Peninsula*

Opposite: *Hector's dolphins typically go in search of food during dives that last only minutes at a time. Like all whales, dolphins get their oxygen from the air through blowholes, like that shown here.*

When Greg Stone is asked why we should care if Hector's dolphins disappear from the earth, he remembers the house he grew up in. "When I was a little kid," he says, "I used to put my ear to the floor of our house, and I would hear all this stuff in the basement. I didn't know what it was. Thinking back on it now, there was probably a water heater, and we lived out in the country so there was probably a water pump, and a washing machine, and a furnace, and all this other noisy stuff down there, but to me it was always the sound of the house's master engine.

"The earth is like your house," he continues. "The house and the pipes, electricity, and pumps that make it livable are like the earth and its biodiversity. You don't understand what happens in your basement but it's vital to your life and your survival. You might not see how everything is connected, but when something goes wrong, or when you lose something down there where you can't see it, it affects the entire house—or in this case, the entire planet. And suddenly your house is not as livable as it was before."

Left: *A researcher gets close to a pair of Hector's dolphins, which sometimes swim close enough to touch.*

Opposite: *Viewing blind at Penguin Place, Otago Peninsula, New Zealand, allows researchers and tourists a glimpse of yellow-eyed penguins through narrow viewing slits.*

Ecotourism and the Yellow-Eyed Penguin

A visitor to Banks Peninsula and Akaroa Harbor will encounter penguins as well as Hector's dolphins. It may seem odd to discover penguins anywhere but in the giant ice fields of the frozen continent called Antarctica, but of the seventeen species of penguins in the world, only six live anywhere near the ice.

Although yellow-eyed penguins occasionally appear on the beaches of Akaroa Harbor, most of their population lives 500 miles and more south: on Stewart, Auckland, and Campbell islands, and on stretches of mainland coast such as the Catlins and the Otago Peninsula. It is here in Otago that a young German student named Hiltrun Ratz has decided to learn everything she can about yellow-eyed penguins. Hiltrun is a graduate student at nearby Otago University, but she works as a part-time guide at Penguin Place, a coastal reserve and sheep farm 20 miles northeast of Dunedin, New Zealand's fifth largest city.

Penguin Place is private farmland owned by Howard and Elizabeth McGrouther. Business partners in the conservation project, Howard McGrouther and Scott Clarke have turned part of their land into an unusual opportunity for tourists to view penguins in their natural habitat—what is called *ecotourism*. Ecotourism in its best sense allows visitors an intimate view of wildlife in a way that does not interfere with the animals' day-to-day lives.

Left: *The outside of a viewing blind at Penguin Place shows the considerable effort used to camouflage the blinds from the penguins.*

Top: *The beach at Penguin Place that tourists are allowed to visit. Another beach nearby is restricted to penguins only.*

Above: *A juvenile penguin shows the soft down on his head—all that remains after the molt of the chick's first coat.*

When ecotourism works as it is supposed to, visitors' fees help fund caretaking of animals that are sick or injured, and the resident animals build nests, bear young, and find protection from predators. Visitors can quietly glimpse rare moments in the natural life cycle of the animal—in the case of Penguin Place, the yellow-eyed penguin. With an increase from eight breeding pairs of penguins in 1985 to thirty-six pairs in 1996, Penguin Place is a very successful example of ecotourism living up to its promise.

On a typical day, Hiltrun Ratz introduces groups of no more than fifteen people to some of the most important facts about the yellow-eyed penguin and its life history. Then she leads them to viewing blinds near the beach. Besides being the world's most endangered penguin—there are thought to be no more than seven thousand in all—yellow-eyed penguins are also one of the species' most solitary and shy. A mere glimpse of a human nearby can send them scurrying for cover.

The habitat yellow-eyed penguins have sought in the past consisted of a forest nest framed by a fallen tree or a thicket of shrubs, sometimes as far as half a mile away from the ocean. Along the coastline around Penguin Place, this kind of nesting habitat has disappeared as people moved into the area and cleared the land for farming and other kinds of development.

As a temporary replacement for protective shrubs until new vegetation can be planted, the caretakers at Penguin Place have built makeshift A-frames, snug hideaways backed by an assortment of bushes to ensure privacy and safekeeping from beasts of prey. Predators such as stoats (a kind of weasel), ferrets (a sort of mink), and feral cats (the wild version of the house cat) are the biggest worry of biologists who are looking to help penguin populations recover. In New Zealand's history, Hiltrun tells visitors, this was not always the case.

Thousands of years ago, New Zealand was penguin heaven. Before the arrival of Polynesians a thousand years ago, now called Maori (MAU-ree), and Europeans 850 years later, flightless birds of every imaginable color and size roamed the islands of New Zealand with few predators in sight. Two species of bats were the only land mammals on the islands. The closest land was Australia, nearly 1,000 miles away.

But with the arrival of human settlers came rats, opossums, and domesticated animals such as cats and dogs that would eventually spell doom for many kinds of flightless birds unaccustomed to such enemies.

Left: *There are fourteen sheep per person in New Zealand. Sheep farming can affect penguin habitat by altering nesting sites and trampling burrows.*

Right: *A makeshift A-frame nesting box is the preferred shelter for yellow-eyed penguins at Penguin Place.*

As Hiltrun continues her description of the plight of the yellow-eyed penguin at Penguin Place, she explains how predators endanger penguins. Because of their size, it isn't the adult penguins that are at risk so much as it is their helpless hatchlings. From the time they hatch to the first year after they leave the nest, the hatchlings are vulnerable. The numbers tell a grim story: Only 48 percent of the birds survive from the time they leave their parents to the time they are one year old.

Yellow-eyed penguins lay two bluish-white eggs four days apart in September, the beginning of spring in New Zealand. While one parent tends to the eggs, the other goes off in search of food. Both penguin parents share egg-incubation duties equally for the six weeks it takes to hatch.

The two furry youngsters that peck their way out of the eggs weigh only about

4 ounces at hatching and are completely dependent on their parents for protection and food. Nearly four months will pass until the chicks lose their furry down and prepare to begin life on their own—February, the time of year Hiltrun leads this morning's tour.

February is the end of summer in New Zealand, and most of the adult penguins are out at sea hunting food for their chicks. Penguin chicks shed their downy feathers throughout January and February as they prepare to go off and be independent of their parents forever. But before they go, they are especially demanding of their parents. Under their mother's and father's care, they grow plump and well nourished. The extra fat reserves they store away now improve their chances of survival while they are learning to hunt on their own.

Right: *A trio of yellow-eyed penguins get playful during the midafternoon at Penguin Place.*

The gathering place for tourists is about a mile inland from the beach next to owner Howard McGrouther's home. Hiltrun explains that there are two beaches side by side at Penguin Place, only one of which is open to tourists. The other, private beach allows Hiltrun and the other scientists to compare the two locations for the impact tourist visits might have on penguin nesting and feeding. From the studies completed so far, the two beaches seem to attract penguins equally and record similar breeding success. That is a good sign for workers at Penguin Place as well as for the tourist who wants to catch a glimpse of penguins in their daily routines.

At the entrance to the reserve itself, a hilltop vista looks down on patchy shrubs ringed by protective fences. Here and there well-camouflaged tunnels, walkways, and viewing huts are visible, like sets from a war movie invasion. Even the viewing huts are painted in the broken shapes and tan and faded green camouflage of army fatigues.

Left: *Penguin Place entry*

Opposite: *Two yellow-eyed penguins move inland to their A-frame shelter.*

The first tunnel leading to a viewing hut begins at the top of a gently sloping hillock. Hiltrun cautions the group she is leading to stay close and quiet to avoid scaring a juvenile that is basking in the midmorning sun beside a nearby A-frame nest. No flash photography is allowed. Sudden bursts of light might frighten the penguins—or even worse, injure their eyes.

Inside the tunnel, visitors walk in single file. Sometimes newly bonded adult penguins feel so comfortable with the network of hidden walkways that they select a nesting site right in the shadow of the camouflage netting. When that happens, Penguin Place caretakers reroute traffic until hatching is successful and complete.

"Every penguin here has a personality," Hiltrun tells the two Japanese and one American who are part of the tour. "Each is banded with a metal ring around the right flipper [marked with a number], and we give them names. So each is known to us, each is protected individually, and each life story is recorded."

Far left: *Opening to a tunnel leading to a viewing blind in Penguin Place*

Left: *Yellow-eyed penguins get rid of their body heat by lifting up their pectoral flippers.*

Opposite: *Tunnel at Penguin Place allows scientists and researchers access to viewing huts without disturbing the penguins in their habitat.*

The network of camouflaged tunnels leads through a maze of turns that pass small rectangular viewing huts with narrow viewing slits. As Hiltrun stops at the final and biggest observation room, she prepares the group for what they are about to see. "In the colony, the penguins are offered nest boxes that provide them with the shelter, shade, and privacy they require for successful breeding," she says. The nest boxes replace the habitat that humans have destroyed over years of land development.

A mix of juveniles and adults are visible 50 feet from the viewing port. Some are resting in the nest boxes Hiltrun talks about while others, mostly the recently fledged juveniles, poke inquisitively around the shrubbery and dunes. They are waiting for the return of their parents who are foraging at sea. When one of the young ones decides to break off from the rest to trudge up a hill close to the tunnel, it gets close enough to reveal a mane of chick down on the top of its head, the only reminder of its hatching four months earlier.

Left: A viewing hut near the crest of a hill overlooks the main beach at Penguin Place.

Above: A sleeping penguin takes shelter from the midday heat in an A-frame.

Opposite: A pair of yellow-eyed penguins frisk about outside their shelter.

First-year juveniles don't yet have the characteristic yellow eyes and head-encircling band. Their irises are gray and will gradually turn yellow during the three to six months after their first molt.

Retracing her steps through the tunnel, Hiltrun then leads the group of human visitors up a hill to another observation hut looking out on a beach and the ocean.

When asked about the future of the yellow-eyed penguin in New Zealand, Hiltrun is positive but says there are lessons to be learned. "The children who are tomorrow's decision makers," she offers, "need to learn that all creatures have to be honored and protected, and that an extinction is a catastrophe that should be prevented at all costs. With every extinction we lose something of our own soul." But by educating people about the fragile ecosystems that surround them, perhaps Hiltrun and others can turn the tide of extinction.

If Penguin Place continues to be successful and to see its penguin population flourish, its kind of responsible ecotourism will have shown that it can help New Zealand's Department of Conservation by making more people aware of the unique wildlife we all stand to lose.

Left: *Penguin Place beach is a gathering place for other wildlife such as fur seals and occasionally Hector's sea lions.*

Opposite: *Vivian Hextall watches two of her little blue penguin patients waddle out into Wellington Harbor for a morning swim.*

Little Blue and Grassroots Conservation

Vivian Hextall lives in a two-story house on the outskirts of the city of Wellington in North Island, New Zealand. She works for IBM full time, but her heart is in the animal care center she runs out of her house on the edge of Wellington Harbor. She founded Eastern Bays Little Blue Penguin Foundation in May 1994, and has been treating injured and sick penguins and other stray animals ever since.

Viv Hextall makes no pretense that she is a savior of all abandoned wildlife. She knows she runs a risk of healing her patients and then having them become so dependent on her care that they can never successfully return to the wild. But she manages those risks by working as closely as she can with veterinarian Steve Robb and representatives of New Zealand's Department of Conservation, who help her band the birds she eventually releases.

Beyond the argument of whether she is really helping the conservation department in its species recovery plans, however, is the community attention she has drawn to the plight of animals that collide with city life. Not only does she enlist the volunteer efforts of neighbors, but she takes her awareness into local schools to help children appreciate the wildlife of the harbor.

In fact, she sees her educational efforts as being as important—if not more important, in some ways—than the rescue work she does with her animals. Through handouts, games, posters, and other specially created materials, she offers children instruction in the basic principles of conservation relating to marine animals and opens their eyes to the plight of the little blue and other animals in and around Wellington.

Above: *Rehabilitation records of the Eastern Bays Little Blue Penguin Foundation*

Left: *The dining room of Viv Hextall's sanctuary is sometimes a refuge for little blue penguins trying to escape the wind and weather. A marker board shows the names of animals currently being treated in the makeshift hospital.*

Above: *The oceanfront shelter of Viv Hextall's hospital home protects two of its patients—Rufus the gull and Trevor the shag.*

On any one day Viv may have as many as ten or more animals in her hospital/home. The Little Blue Penguin Foundation consists of a fenced-in garden in front of the house and a patio and gazebo facing the ocean. Patients might include Rufus, the gull with the broken wing; Trevor, a cormorant-like seabird called a spotted shag; and Albie, the little blue penguin. Each animal gets a daily dose of medications, food, and tender loving care as Viv takes them on their way to rehabilitation and release.

Little blue penguins are the smallest penguin species in the world, less than a foot tall, about the size of the average guinea pig. There are thought to be as many as five subspecies of little blue penguins that live in New Zealand and among its outlying islands stretching to Australia. A subspecies is a very closely related species that has lived apart from its cousins, often separated by great distances for long periods of time. The little blue penguin subspecies from Australia, for example, is called a fairy penguin. Here in Wellington, New Zealand, the variety of little blue has a darker blue coloration than the little blue from New Zealand's southern islands.

Little blues are not endangered birds in New Zealand—at least not yet. But they often make nests near roadways, and they are so small that even adult little blues are vulnerable to domestic animals such as dogs. These two facts alone may yet bring them to be declared a threatened species, especially as humans keep crowding the coasts.

Opposite: *Viv Hextall goes through her morning routine of hand-feeding the birds and then letting them out for a swim.*

Below: *Viv carries the more delicate little blue penguins out for their morning swim, while more robust little blues make their own way.*

A typical day in Viv Hextall's daily schedule will end with food preparation just before bedtime. She takes fish she has recently purchased—cod, gurnard, Hoki, and herring—out of the freezer to get ready for the following morning's feed. Then, just before sunrise, she takes the little blue penguins, often two at a time, down a ladder to send them off for a morning swim.

It doesn't take long, however, before the early morning swimmers choose to return to their backyard sanctuary, climbing up a wooden plank that leads to a tunnel made of PVC pipe.

Above: *Viv Hextall hand carries a penguin down a ladder from her backyard sanctuary to the ocean below.*

Left: *Once the little blue penguins have finished their swim they waddle up a wooden platform (of their own choice) and reenter the animal care beachfront hospital through a specially designed PVC pipe.*

Above: *Fresh from a morning dip, a little blue penguin rests briefly outside the scupper entrance before making its way back to the relative warmth of the beachfront hospital.*

Individual penguins are hand-fed. Since many of them are thin and dehydrated, Viv takes special care to make sure they get enough food and the necessary vitamins and antibiotics they need to survive. Some of her charges are so skinny after their rescue, they will do anything they can to sneak into the house for the warmth of a wall-to-wall carpet and protection from the wind.

The rescue and release of a little blue penguin named Albie is probably Viv Hextall's favorite story. Albie was discovered on the twenty-sixth of February, 1995, and weighed just 700 grams, or 24.7 ounces. The victim of an oil spill, Albie was covered from head to toe in thick black oil. He was a juvenile penguin, probably in his first two years of life and with no obvious injuries. The loose skin on his body, however, showed him to be very underweight and perilously close to death.

Excerpts from Viv's carefully kept records of Albie's stay in her care tell the story best, and reveal how difficult and delicate an animal rescue is.

Entries from Viv's journal are followed by explanations of her actions and definitions of some journal terms.

Treatment Details

2/26/95

4 P.M. Bird caught on Day's Bay beach. Minimum stress catch; Rosalie walked straight up to it and threw a damp towel over it. Very little resistance to being handled.

Rosalie is Viv Hextall's partner in the Eastern Bays Little Blue Penguin Foundation. She discovered Albie on a beach in Wellington Harbor. Albie was sick and weak, and Rosalie used a damp towel to capture him. The towel protected her from being pecked and made it easier for her to carry Albie back to Viv's house for treatment.

4:05 P.M. Fed 1/2 Titralac tablet and 0.3ml glucose mixture orally by syringe to start flushing system and reduce shock.

Titralac is an antacid, like Pepto-Bismol or Tums. Many of the birds Viv and Rosalie rescue are starved and weak, and since the Titralac tablet is bitter, they give the penguins their pills along with a sugar/glucose solution. The sugar helps the medicine go down and gives the birds a quick boost of energy.

4:10 P.M. Bird placed in a bucket of warm water with feet touching bottom, and the washing began. Used Sards Wonder Soap and Flex Extra Body Balsam and Protein shampoo. Soap massaged into body and water changed frequently to get rid of excess oil. A very slow and painstaking job! Cleaned most of the oil off within 3-hour period using 175 ml shampoo and 1/2 cake of soap. Oil difficult to remove from around facial area as we did not want to get soap in eyes. Bird rinsed under warm shower and put in plastic tub to swim rest out. The bird was very cooperative during this time but started to get very cold.

Wrapped in a warm towel and held till he heated up and then placed into a cage with a warm hot-water bottle wrapped in a towel. Bird lay down and went to sleep.

Albie was covered with oil from the harbor, so Viv and Rosalie tried to wash the oil off with soap and shampoo. But penguins depend on the oil they produce from special glands to make them waterproof and to keep them warm, and unfortunately removing the harbor oil meant removing all the bird's oil, exposing him to the cold. So to keep Albie's temperature up, they placed a hot-water bottle in his cage.

3/1/95 (three days later)

10:30 P.M. Bathroom looks like a bomb has hit it. Penguin had been swimming in his "pond" and there was water everywhere. Albie was soaking wet. Cleaned up mess with Albie happily preening in the middle of the mayhem.

Viv's bathroom tub serves as a temporary ocean for Albie while he is recovering. The tub water can be kept warmer than the ocean and keeps the penguin free from danger of freezing. By now Albie has begun to use his oil glands when he preens his feathers—that is, he rubs the oil his glands produce on his feathers to make himself waterproof.

3/2/95

6:15 A.M. Cleaned bathroom—not so messy this morning. Albie had been swimming again. Now begging for food. Flippers out from body pointing sharply backwards. Fed 100 grms cod with Vibravet antibiotic.

Viv uses the color of the skin on a bird's feet and its behavior—whether it acts tired or listless—to help her judge the penguin's health. A bird that shows little curiosity or movement and has red or swollen feet suggests it might be running a fever. Viv gives Albie Vibravet, an antibiotic that comes as a chocolate-flavored paste. Probably because of the sweet taste, it is easy to feed a penguin Vibravet.

3/7/95

11:45 A.M. [notes entered by Ineke, a volunteer] Noisy welcome. Ate ravenously—dipped briefly, which he objected to. Insisted on coming inside, swore at me—I like him!

3/9/95

1:30 P.M. Got up because of the racket. When I opened the door he literally fell inside and rocketed off to the seaside door. Was in a very ratty mood and pecked me when I tried to pick him up. He is definitely moving towards more independent behavior—even slightly aggressive.

Albie's feisty behavior is a sign that he is returning to good health. Since Viv's living room is not Albie's normal home, he is showing signs that he wants to get back to the wild.

8:30 P.M. Heard Albie pecking at the door, wanting to be fed. Fed 170 grms cod and gurnard with salt and put him outside after preening him for a while. Weighed 1,200 grms [42.3 ounces].

Albie weighed only 700 grams (24.7 ounces) when Rosalie first found him on the beach, so his weight gain and enthusiasm for eating is a good sign. Cod and gurnard are fish the penguins like that are available from local markets. Ineke "preens" Albie by scratching him and encouraging him to preen himself.

3/10/95

8:00 A.M. Fed 50 grms cod and gave him a swim. Still not very water-proof; we will not be able to let him go this weekend.

Besides appetite, one of Viv's biggest concerns is waterproofing of the feathers. Although Albie has begun preening, he still hasn't spread enough oil into his feathers for him to survive in the ocean.

7:30 P.M. Banded by Dave Bell [a volunteer]—"Looks healthy and ready to be released." Measurements taken: Bill length 34.9 mm. Bill depth 13.0 mm.

3/18/95

4:30 P.M. Let run around seaside yard—quite happy; is getting very good at balance and climbing activity now. Fed 100 grms Hoki and salt. Gave a brief swim—belly still not waterproof yet.

Hoki is another penguin favorite at Viv's place—and happily for her, relatively inexpensive and easy to find at the supermarket.

3/23/95

1:45 P.M. [entry by Ineke] He welcomed me with open flippers and much quacking. He had been listening to the Rolling Stones last night and was fatigued he informs me. I reckon he's in robust good health, just bored. Doesn't do a blind thing all day—doesn't get tired out. He needs an Outward Bound course. Fed 90 grms Hoki and pinch of salt.

Ineke's discovery of a listless Albie is not a good sign for a successful release.

3/28/95

6:45 A.M. Scupper training went well but he had the shakes again today. Didn't push him. He was in his kennel at first light and came out only when he saw the food dish. Fed 110 grms Hoki and salt. Came through the scupper hole without being called.

The scupper is a large plastic pipe that connects Viv's waterfront porch with the ocean. It allows water to wash in and drain out to the harbor but is also used by the penguins to come and go in the yard as they please. Scupper training is Viv's attempt to get the birds comfortable with the scupper, with coming and going—eventually for good.

12:00 P.M. [entry by Ineke] Fed 100 grms Hoki and salt. Well taken. Happy to go back into the kennel.

6:30 P.M. Scupper training—not very hungry this evening; more interested in investigating than eating. Ate 60 grms Hoki and salt. Tried fresh herring but he spat this out. Didn't want to come through the scupper at the end—turned around to head back to the beach. First overt sign that he is ready to leave.

Viv tries to interest Albie in fresh herring because it is more like the food he will find in the wild.

Given a swim in the pool to encourage fitness. Lots of ducking, diving, and preening. Should be able to release him tomorrow if the weather is fine.

3/29/95

Somewhat apprehensive this morning—shaking evident. Shot into the bathroom at the first opportunity. Put outside into the kennel.

Viv does not want Albie to get used to the bathroom for protection—especially so close to release time. The kennel—a plastic box like those used to transport pets on airplanes—protects Albie somewhat from the cold and the surf but still gives him a feel for the outside elements he'll have to face when he's back in the world.

1:00 P.M. [entry by Ineke] *Got no welcome. Had to look inside kennel. He was a bit reluctant to follow me to the scupper, so he was carried. Then refused to have anything to do with 1/2 pilchard. Ate 100 grms Hoki and salt and hurried back to his quarters. No thank you or anything. I have cut him out of my will.*

6:40 p.m. Wandered out of his kennel and arrived in the seaside yard. Weighed 1,150 grms. Fed 2 small herrings whole, 100 grms Hoki, 1/2 Mazun, and 1/2 pilchard. Very cooperative feeding. Released this evening.

Albie's weight when first discovered was 700 grams (24.7 ounces); his weight appears to have balanced out at an optimum weight of 1,150–1,200 grams (40.6–42.3 ounces). He eats one last meal with Viv and then is ready to go.

Release Details

3/29/95

Released—scupper left open after feeding. We turned him to face it so that he realized that he was free to go if he wished. After 10 minutes he went through and stood for about 5 minutes on the top step— orientation. He is familiar with the platform. He took the shortest route down to the water's edge and swam around—ducking, diving, and rolling in the immediate vicinity for 10 minutes. Disappeared from sight at 8:10 P.M. Albie can always return if he needs to.

Another success story for the Eastern Bays Little Blue Penguin Foundation—but the end of Albie's treatment is just one part of what Viv Hextall must accomplish to make certain he and others like him are safe. The greater task is educating people in the area about the real dangers of pollution and urban development. Human-caused environmental hazards are the biggest danger to the little blues. If enough people are thinking about the little blues and other coastal-dwelling animals, perhaps one day Viv's hospital won't be necessary anymore.

But until that day she'll continue to do her work.

Conclusion

In the waters of New Zealand, little blue penguins still have the choice to return to nests in shoreline caves and fishing grounds just off the coast. Unlike the yellow-eyed penguin and Hector's dolphin, their population numbers are still high enough not to be in immediate threat of extinction. The awareness of where and how little blues live, however—even through the small window that Viv Hextall's rescue operation provides into the daily lives of her dependents—may eventually help to protect them if their populations ever do get threatened. The hundreds of local schoolchildren who learn about the plight of the little blue through school outreach programs may someday be the difference between public indifference and community support. Already the school outreach programs have made a difference in the lives of the little blues.

While Viv Hextall's Eastern Bays Little Blue Penguin Foundation educates people in her area about what can be done for little blues, Penguin Place introduces the lives of endangered yellow-eyed penguins to an even wider public—local and international. People are drawn from all over the world to see this kind of penguin found nowhere else, and the experience they have at Penguin Place may make them more sympathetic to wildlife in danger in their own backyards. Penguin Place also plays an important support role to the Department of Conservation's public outreach efforts. The Department of Conservation is busy trying to save animal habitats, and its members work with limited funds to look after the most severely endangered animals such as the black robin, once reduced to a single breeding pair but now on the rebound. Programs such as that at Penguin Place make it easier for conservationists to get funding by raising general awareness.

And awareness is what makes the difference between whether we allow the animals of our coasts to be driven out and made extinct—or whether we take care to live harmoniously with our world. Carelessness and ignorance will mean an inevitable slide toward extinction for these animals.

Hector's dolphins, yellow-eyed penguins, and little blue penguins can still find fishing grounds and undisturbed natural habitat for nests—but that may not always be the case as human population grows and natural habitat disappears. Because what is happening in New Zealand has already happened in many of the more developed and densely populated countries around the world, New Zealand has a preview of what it must try to avoid. From government conservation to backyard sanctuaries, New Zealanders have shown they are skilled at finding ways to preserve their biodiversity while it is still possible. More importantly, they have made it clear that with careful research and attention and luck, it is almost always possible to accommodate the needs of coastal wildlife—and that our lives and the lives of future generations will be far richer as a result.

A Glossary of Some Terms Used in This Book

Biodiversity. Another way of saying "biological diversity," a measure of the different life forms in a particular area, including a variety of plant and animal species.

Dolphin. A member of a group of over thirty species of relatively small, toothed whales, whose most familiar representatives are the bottlenose and spinner dolphins. Dolphins usually have cone-shaped teeth and beaks, unlike porpoises, which have spade-shaped teeth and no beak. Dolphins come from the family of whales called Delphinidae, while porpoises are in the family Phocoenidae. The terms *dolphin, porpoise,* and *whale* are not always clear: See the sidebar on page 12.

Ecotourism. A way of combining tourism with conservation. Tourists are allowed to view wildlife in situations where care is taken not to disturb the animals in their natural surroundings and where the tourist money helps protect and maintain the animals' natural habitat.

Endangered species. According to the IUCN/World Conservation Union, *endangered species* are species "in danger of extinction and whose survival is unlikely if the causal factors continue operating." The black rhinoceros and the Kemp's ridley sea turtle are examples of species identified by the IUCN/World Conservation Union as endangered.

Fledgling. A bird that has grown the feathers necessary for flying. In the case of a penguin, a fledgling is a young bird that has replaced its downy feathers with feathers that will allow it to swim and keep warm in the water.

Gill nets. These are called set nets in New Zealand. Gill nets allow fish to swim into an opening in the net only as far as their gills and no farther. Once trapped in the net's opening or mesh, their gills catch in the net and won't let the fish back out.

Glucose. Sugar in crystal form, obtained from fruits and honey.

Habitat. The environment in which a specified animal typically lives. One of the habitats for the yellow-eyed penguin, for example, used to be forest shrubbery near the coast.

Hector's dolphin. A kind of dolphin that lives only in and around New Zealand waters and which is one of the rarest species of dolphins in the world.

Maori. Native peoples of New Zealand whose ancestors came from Polynesia, arriving by boat in New Zealand about a thousand years ago.

Molt. The process by which a bird sheds one layer of feathers and replaces it with another layer of feathers.

Pinger. A device that makes pinging sounds—brief bursts of high-pitched noises. It is used by whale researchers to alert dolphins and other marine mammals to the presence of fishing nets.

Porpoise. A member of a group of six species of relatively small, toothed whales, in the family Phocoenidae that have spade-shaped teeth and no beak.

Radio tag. A device to let scientists keep track of the movements of animals. Attached to the dorsal fin of a whale, for example, this kind of tag sends VHF radio signals to the scientists' receiver radios whenever its antenna breaks the surface of the water.

Scupper. An opening cut through the waterway and bulwarks of a ship, so that water falling on deck may flow overboard; an opening in the wall of a building to permit water to drain off a floor or flat roof.

Set nets. See *gill nets.*

Sonar. A device that transmits high-frequency sound waves through water and then detects the vibrations that are reflected back. Sonar can locate a school of fish or a whale, for example, and measure how far away they are.

Species. A group of animals related by descent, able to breed among themselves but not with other organisms.

Spotted shag. A marine bird from the cormorant family. Shags and cormorants are able to swim underwater to catch fish because their feathers absorb water, making them less buoyant.

Subspecies. A population of a species distinguished from other such populations by having a different genetic makeup, usually the result of living in a different geographic range.

Threatened. This term is used to describe animals protected by the World Conservation Union but which are not yet classified as *endangered.* The little blue penguin is currently on the list of threatened species.

Viewing blind. A place where people can view wildlife without being seen. A viewing blind can be a carefully camouflaged hut with slits for looking out or a makeshift visual barrier.

More Books about Dolphins and Penguins

Dolphin Man: Exploring the World of Dolphins by Laurence Pringle. Atheneum Books for Young Readers, 1995.

Sea World Book of Penguins by Frank Todd. Sea World Press/Harcourt Brace Jovanovich, 1981.

The Hoiho: New Zealand's Yellow-Eyed Penguin by Adele Vernon. Putnam, 1991.

Whales, Dolphins, and Porpoises by Mark Carwardine. Eyewitness Handbooks, Dorling Kindersley, 1992.